To Heaven and Back With Angels

Timothy Peak

Disclaimer

To Heaven and Back With Angels

Dedications

I dedicate this book to all the people seeking comfort from the loss of a loved one and those who question the power of God's love for us all.

Contents

Chapter 1: My Life before Everything Changed

Let me introduce myself before I relate the life-altering experience that I have had. My name is Timothy Peak. Most of my friends and loved ones call me Tim. I am a 54 year-old male and still love my wife, Kandice, of 35 years. She is 53 now and the mother of our 4 sons. Timothy, the eldest, is 34, then there is Jordan who is 28, Spencer who is 26-years-old, and finally, Tyler who's just 15.

We hail from New Castle, PA where we have lived all our lives. However, we frequently visit Beaufort SC. and enjoy our time there.

We had spent much time together growing up and enjoying the outdoors. All the kids loved hunting and fishing. We spent many weekends together at Pymatuning state park where they also enjoyed swimming and learning to ride their bikes as my parents had done with me and my brothers and sister when we were kids. We have many good memories from those past days and still today we camp and boat there.

It is an amazing place for raising kids. Our family returned with fond memories of cooking hot dogs and roasting marshmallows on the fire at dusk. The darker it gets, the brighter the fire gets and the bigger their little eyes get with excitement and wonder. And who wouldn't like a boat ride on the lake with the hopes of catching a big walley?

We had spent many hours in the woods, picking different kinds of eatable plants and fruits. It would start off in the spring around the middle of May, when the May Apples would just start to become riddled throughout the woods. My wife and I would take our kids out and pick morale mushrooms and bring them back to the house, rinse them off, and let them soak in water.

In the meanwhile, we would then go to the creek to catch trout until we had a half dozen or so. Then we would bring them home to cook with the mushrooms and a side dish of dandelions that we would pick on our way back to the truck from fishing.

We lived nearby to a stream called Neshannock Creek. It is regularly stocked with trout by the Pennsylvania Fish Commission. The first day of trout is usually around April 15th. So, it falls right into play with all the other outdoor events that are happening at this time of the year. Then we would go spring turkey hunting. This opening day usually happens around the last week of April or the first week of May.

In the spring, you can harvest the male bird only. The male turkey is called a gobbler. We have harvested a few of these birds but there have been years that we came home empty handed. We would spend many mornings in the woods trying to call in one of these witty birds.

My kids always loved the spring because to them, that's when all the outdoor excitement happened here in our area of western Pennsylvania. I always tried to teach them the full beauty of nature and to respect what God has given us to enjoy.

At this time of the season, we would then travel some 40 miles north pulling a small fishing boat to Pymatuning State Park to fish for walley from the boat. My kids have many good memories, spent floating on this lake in the chilly mornings.

At this time of the year, it isn't quite time to camp yet, we all knew it was just around the corner. About a few weeks after this, we would switch from walley fishing to crappie fishing at a different lake called Sharpsville Reservoir, located in Hermitage Pa.

We really enjoyed these lakes. They are around 30 miles apart and the towns that surround these lakes have a calming air about them. In both these areas, reside a community of Amish people and they are always found enjoying the outdoors and the tranquility that it provides. It is quite fascinating to watch these people with their simplest manner of living and enjoying life. Here is their horse buggy to show for such a simple manner of living:

We became friends with some of them and I really got to enjoy the opportunity of taking them fishing with us, and they seem to enjoy fishing with us. The whole experience felt as if we have traveled back in time, almost 100 years back. Those kids were funny and we laughed the entire time that we fished.

We also took our kayaks to both of these lakes and enjoyed the soothing scenery. As usual, my son Tyler, brought one of his friends so that they can do their own thing.

My wife and I would hope for me to be able to take time from my busy schedule and spend the day with the kids and a bucket of minnows along the shores catching this tasty little fish. There is nothing in this world more exciting to a young child catching his first fish or for that matter many, many fish. It gives a sense of accomplishment as a parent to help and witness this special event taking place.

I really didn't know who was more excited for their master feat at the moment, me or them. Ha this is life!

My kids are starting their own families now, and already making plans to purchase campers and boats of their own. They want to teach their kids what they themselves have experienced in the outdoors. We really love camping under the palm trees right on the beach about 20 yards away from the ocean on Hunting Island, at Beaufort County in South Carolina. It is so beautiful and exciting there.

Sometimes we would pull our camper there, and at other times, we would stay in a tent right on the beach. It is about a 14 hour drive from where we live in Pennsylvania, so sometimes, the tent is an easier option. Considering, we only sleep, and wake up, and leave for the day. The tent is a practical idea. We love staying there because when you camp at this state park, there are many benefits. Not just because you can fall to sleep listening to the soft waves rolling onto the beach or waking up and stepping into the soft sand right out the door and smelling the clean salty air.

They have educational seminars for sea turtles that make their nests right in front of you, 20 yards away from the ocean on Hunting Island state park. These nest areas are watched and monitored by the park rangers, and if you are lucky enough, you will see a hatch taking place. Unfortunately, we haven't witnessed that spectacular event yet, but, maybe in the future, we will.

When you pay for admission to stay at this very large island, you are given free access to all the events. These include an unlimited access to the fishing pier that is located about a half mile down the road. The fishing pier has a museum that features all the local fish, birds, and animals in the area. They have something different there every time we go.

My kids love to see the turtles and the snakes in the museum, and the rangers that work there are more than happy to talk to you, and give you any kind of information you want about the animals. We have a couple metal detectors, and we try to make time to go up and down the beach once or twice a day while trying to find objects that are of historical origins.

We haven't found anything of true value in the money sense, but we do find things that are still a mystery of what they are.

There is a museum in the city of Beaufort of all the valuable artifacts, which consist of gold coins and cannon balls from the years past. About another mile down the road, they have a wooden dock that extends about a half mile into the marsh waters. We would park under the palm trees next to the many palmettos that riddle this area. Then, we would carry our casting nets and head to the end of this marsh walk to throw them into the water and place our crab traps at the end of this beautiful structure. We do that in the hopes of filling a cooler with shrimp and blue crabs.

They built a beautiful gazebo on this walk in the middle of the marsh. We sit under the roof and enjoy the beautiful nature that surrounds us. This structure is built just above the marsh and when the tide is out, there are millions of small crabs that catch your attention. You could spend hours alone watching these little creatures competing for their spots in the mud.

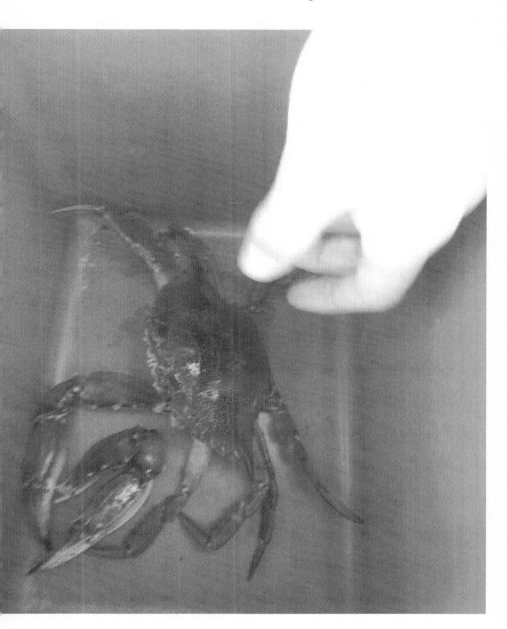

Then there is a very old lighthouse on the island that the locals are very proud of. There is a beautiful park that surrounds this old lighthouse just yards away from the beach. They have picnic shelters and tables and walkways throughout this area.

For a small fee, you can go to the top of this lighthouse and admire the breathtaking view of this area. My wife and kids adventure up this structure every time we visit this place. I sit on the bench and wait for them.

That's because I really don't like heights, so I would rather sit on the bench with my feet planted on solid ground. We would then travel into the historic city of Beaufort to get something to eat. There is always something interesting to see on our drive there. Whether it is the beautiful boats or the drawbridge that we must cross to get from one island to another, there is always an eye-catching view.

After we eat at one of the many places to choose from, we will then go to another small secluded spot that we frequent called Pigeon Point. It is a small area at the end of a dead end road that has a small boat launch and a small pier that extends into the marsh. It is open to the public.

One evening, we were there, and a small group of people showed up with the intentions of witnessing a glimpse of the space shuttle that was traveling over this area shortly. We sat in our chairs and waited while watching the stars on this cloudless night. The stars were just beautiful and it was very warm out. We sat for about an hour before we had finally seen this shuttle. We continued to watch for about an hour before it was out of sight. It was a very interesting event for all of us.

During the day, in this area, we like to throw our cast nets for shrimp and enjoy watching the dolphins swimming around us. The locals in this area love to see the dolphins, and it seems that the aquatic mammals know they are being looked at as very special and loved creatures. They like to broadcast their presence with loud puffs of air through their blow holes. They will swim very close as if they were saying, hello, here I am! How are you doing today?

My son Tyler likes to stand on this small aluminum boat dock and catch small black tip sharks with his fishing pole. He learned this from a local man named John. He was fascinated with catching these interesting fish, and he couldn't wait to come home and tell everyone about his interesting and exciting fishing adventure!

From here, we would go to a place we frequent in Port Royal called Sands Beach. They have a very large fishing pier that runs parallel with the beach and it is about a quarter mile long. At the end of this pier, there is a structure built about 3 stories high where you can go to the top and gaze at the breathtaking views of the ocean. People gather at the shores of this area and look for shark teeth and dig for clams along the water's edge. It is a very interesting place to visit.

One day, Tyler was throwing his casting net off this pier and pulled in a very large mantis shrimp. It was about 8 inches in length and 2 inches wide. He carried it over to me and asked what it was.

Even though it was a very beautiful creature, I didn't have an answer for him because I had no idea what it was. It was transparent and had many beautiful colors throughout its body. We were standing there admiring this beautiful creature when a local fisherman passing by had stopped and explained the whole story about this thing he had just caught.

After the man left, Tyler asked me what to do with it and he decided to put it back into the water.

I am a very private person and really don't enjoy expressing my personal experiences. I spent each day thinking about my quick visit to heaven for 10 years. During that time, many people told me to write a book.

I finally decided to do so with the help and encouragement from a couple priests at my church. This is something that I must do and what the angel had requested from me to do. Tell as many people as I can about my visit to the heavenly kingdom she had said. A book would be a good way to do that.

So, here it is. I hope it will help someone or answer any questions that people might have regarding heaven and our true purpose on earth.

People who know me will tell you that I have always been a hard worker. One of my earliest occupations was that of a construction contractor. It was during that job that I built my own ranch home on 11 acres of property with the help of my father. His name is Walter. He was always involved with me no matter what the situation was, he was always committed to helping me. He is a very special person. And I am very proud of him. Soon, I also became the owner of a couple of rental homes.

Later, I worked as a heavy equipment operator at a local steel mill. But I hadn't stop dabbling in real estate, which is why I also came to own an 11 unit apartment building. I ran and maintained it on my own.

As you can see, so far I had lived an extremely busy life. It all began when I was building a garage and had to stop and take my son Spencer to the orthodontist to get his braces adjusted. Since the orthodontist was about 40 miles away, I had to be absent from my job, and leave my workers and travel with him.

While on our way to the orthodontist, I noticed that it was a rather beautiful August day in 2009. On the way home from there, my truck had begun making a noise. Of course, I wanted to stop before getting on the turnpike, and make sure the truck was going to be alright before beginning the drive home. Thus, I pulled over and popped the hood. When I bent over to look at the engine, I realized to my horror that something was very, very wrong. But it wasn't the truck. It was me; I was blind!

My sight had been taken from me instantaneously. One moment, I could see well enough to open the truck door, get out, and walk to the hood. As soon as I bent over it though, blindness struck me. The fear of the unknown got me very scared very quickly.

I rubbed my eyes thinking that maybe something had gotten into my eyes. You see, I was hoping that when I finished, my vision would have returned. It didn't! At that point, I had noticed that my heart was pounding very fast and I was sweating. I didn't know what was happening to me, but I suspected that I was having a stroke or a heart attack.

Just then Spencer asked, "What's wrong with your eyes, Dad?"

I could tell by the tone of his voice that my son was frightened by something. I didn't want to add to his fear, so I turned my head away. When I was sure he couldn't see me, I went to walk away from him. But my legs refused to budge. Losing my balance, I used an arm on the fender of the truck to hold myself up.

By then, I was very frightened and knew something was seriously wrong. I knew of an auto body shop that was located just across the street.

Still making sure that I was facing the other way, I spoke to my son, "There's something wrong with dad Spencer. Go across the street and tell them I need help."

After Spencer had gone, I just moved my arm because I could not hold myself up for a second longer. Immediately, I fell to the ground. I felt around with my hand until I found the front tire of the truck. Once I did, I labored to sit up and lean against. After a few minutes, I heard footsteps headed my way.

Next, a man asked me "What's wrong?"

I realized that I didn't have a clue, so I replied that I didn't know.

"I cannot see or move my legs," I added.

These people, for he had more men with him, carried me across the street and back to their garage. From there, they called an ambulance and I waited there still blind to the world for 20 minutes. It wasn't until I heard the sirens getting closer to me that I knew that the ambulance had arrived.

Would they be able to help me, I wondered? The paramedics asked me what was wrong again. I told him the same thing but this time I also added that I could feel my heart fluttering really fast. The men were professionals and in constant contact with the nearest hospital. That happened to be the Beaver Valley in Aliquippa PA.

They put me into the ambulance and rushed me there. When I reached the hospital, I was still blind, but more than that I was also confused and scared. A CAT scan and 20 min later, a doctor came into the room where I was. In a grave voice, he asked me if I had any family. I told him about them, which was when he shook his head and told me how sorry he was.

My heart sank as I heard him tell me that I had a brain tumor. My symptoms, according to the doctor, were because it had burst open, filling my brain with blood.

While it had quit bleeding, it had left the doctors puzzled. They didn't know why it bled in the first place any more than they knew why it had quit bleeding. He also told me that they were in the process of calling my family. But then came the sucker punch. The doctor told me they could not do anything for me, and I was going to die.

They had also contacted the professionals at West Penn Hospital in Pittsburgh. By the time my family arrived, I was laying back in a hospital bed still in the emergency room... I had taken some medicine that brought some of my vision back. My eyes could just make out the grids in the ceiling. Sensing a presence, I turned my head to a side and saw a shadowy shape walking back and forth. My father was here, and he had just been told of my devastating situation.

I realized then the doctor was still holding my hand and had been the entire time. Trying to be helpful, he said he could get a deacon to come in and talk to me. I shook my head and told him that I was Catholic; I don't need to speak to anyone. I lay there for an hour with the doctor still holding my hand.

They kept coming into the room, asking me if I had a will, about 6 times. They thought that it would be a good idea to make a living will. I told them that I had already made a will. Even so, they brought up the matter about 6 times. It only made things scarier for me. But I took a deep breath and told myself that if I made a living will, it meant accepting that I was going to end up at the hospital waiting to die. I wasn't ready for that yet. Instead, I chose to fight and win!

My phone rang and I instinctively reached into my pocket and retrieved it for a brief conversation. One of the guys from my job had called because he had been wondering what was taking me so long. I told him I will be there soon before I hung up.

The doctor was shaking his head. "Tim you have to tell them you're not going to come back," he said.

I found myself thinking, what did it matter? They would find out soon enough. Then the doctor left the room, which was when the miracle in my life began.

I was looking at my shoes... at the holes in them. My head had formed the thought that, my goodness, I'm always so busy working, I don't even have time to buy a pair of shoes. These insignificant thoughts usually hit us at highly inopportune moments.

At that time, I was very, very, upset because my life was over and all I could think of was about the holes in my shoes. It wasn't the footwear really, but the idea that all I had done was work. No matter how much time we spend on earth, we never realize what we should have done or could do if we had more time. I had fully understood the saying when people say life is short.

I understood this more profoundly at this point in my life because now I was laying here waiting to die. Life is much, much shorter than we realize and we should all live this life as if every day was our last, because it just may be our last. I really thought I had gotten ripped off in life. Now it was all over (for me) and I was going to die.

Just then a prayer played upon my lips. I closed my eyes and said okay God, here it is. I have absolutely nothing to offer you at this stage of my life. All I have is my word. Now, I'm not afraid to die, but I just don't want to do it now. I want to see my kids grow up and I want to do things differently in my life.

Please let me live and I will be a better person. I won't lie, cheat, steal, or deceive people – not that I did that before, but I had nothing else to say or offer Him. I wasn't finished with my life and I told God if he let me live, I would do so as a better person. At that moment, like I said, I didn't know what else to say to him.

Just then, the doctor returned into the room with 2 other doctors. I heard them talking about why I was still alive. To hear them tell it, the last 5 people that this had happened to were dead by this time. The doctor remained in the room for another 4 hours. Throughout the ordeal, he held my hand. He really did care about his patients.

I don't remember a time when I hadn't been surrounded by very special people in my life. My family was always close and caring. I was truly blessed when it comes to kids.

When my kids were born, I was the happiest man on the planet. I have always loved babies and small children and to have a family of my own, and these babies that were mine, was just amazing to me.

Like all parents think of their own children, mine were very beautiful and special. I couldn't ask for a better life that God had given me. I knew that I was very blessed. And I had made sure that they knew it too!

Then the doctor got a phone call from his counterpart in Pittsburgh. They wanted to bring me there. I was told that if my tumor started to bleed again, I was going to die instantly. Knowing that only God could help me now, I kept the prayer I had uttered in the hospital at the forefront of my mind. I didn't just want to live for myself. My family was a big part of why I wanted to stick around for as long as I could.

When they had come in to see me, I could see how the sad news had ravaged their peace of mind. My wife's pain was visible in her face. She took my hand quietly and shook her head when I tried to apologize. I wasn't saying sorry because this was my fault in any way. No, I didn't blame myself for the tumor. However, I had wanted to apologize for putting my family through this pain.

My sons, the two youngest, looked lost. They didn't understand how life could have changed within a day so drastically. Since I was dealing with my own acceptance issues, my elder sons had stepped in. They hinted to their younger siblings on how to behave and to keep it together. I saw it in the slight nudges they would give or how they would place a reassuring hand on one of their younger brothers' shoulders. My chest swelled up with pride for all of them. They were doing their best to be brave. I took heart that my wife and I had raised them right.

When they brought me to Pittsburgh in another ambulance, I met a very special doctor there. I do believe that he is a gift to us from God. His name is Doctor Howard Senter and has been blessed with a sliver of the Divine power to heal others. Senter doesn't squander his gift and helps people get better or at least pass their last days in comfort.

He is a neurosurgeon, and I could tell from the second that I met him that he was special. He is also very smart, and you'd realize that when you talk to him. While Senter is on a mission to save people's lives, I don't think even he realizes that he is doing God's work.

He just does it because he thinks he can improve the lives of others. As we encountered each other for the first time, I felt as if he was the one that God wanted me to be with. I have yet to ask him what his own first thoughts were.

Doctor Senter told me that this was going to be very difficult. I already knew that, but his warning didn't discourage me in the least.

I chose to focus on what he wasn't saying as opposed to the words coming out of his mouth. If the going would be hard, it didn't mean that it was impossible. Senter asked me to be strong and I took that to mean that he could see there was some fight left in me.

When he said, he would do everything in his power to save my life, I told myself that this man was on a mission. And he was going to give it his ultimate best. Wow! Maybe, I was going to live, I thought.

Before the surgery took place, Senter explained the whole procedure to me. The way he answered my questions filled me with even more confidence about his abilities. He seemed to know what he was doing and that is all the reassurance you and I can ask for. Right?

Dr. Senter did the operation, which consisted of removing the top of my head, and cleaning the blood out. While doing all that, he had also removed 2 tumors called Vascular Angiomas.

Needless to say, I hadn't even known I had one let alone two. I never had had any headaches and had been perfectly healthy my whole entire life. How do you even tell whether you have an abnormal growth taking valuable real estate in your head? One day you have no clue and the next you end up at a hospital. I couldn't believe what had happened to me!

But my family stayed by my side through the entire ordeal. That included my mother who was saying the rosary in the waiting room when I was in surgery. Her name is Carol. She is all Italian and loves to keep her family close. She does this by cooking food. Every Sunday she cooks and the entire family will go to my parents' house to eat dinner and catch up with each other on all the events happening in the family. She is an amazing woman and the greatest cook. She is the last generation in our family to show everyone the Italian tradition. She is also very positive about praying.

There is an unbelievable part that I haven't gotten to yet. Yes, the surgery and the successful removal of not one but two tumors is commendable and sounds unreal.

However, it isn't the only surprising thing that went on that day. Because during my surgery, things suddenly became more interesting. That was when I began seeing a light at the end of a very long dark tunnel.

Since I had been given local anesthesia, I was completely out during surgery. As the tunnel loomed in front of my eyes, I tried to sense if I was the only one who could see it.

Apparently, it was just for me because Dr. Senter kept working on my brain unperturbed by the opening that had just visualized in his place of business. So, did the nurses and the other medical staff that was supposed to be present during my surgery. I had an overwhelming urge to go to this light. I knew instinctively this is where I must go now.

Chapter 2: The Transition

The dark tunnel that only I could spot was about three feet in diameter. The tunnel was completely silent as it hovered in the air above me. It was very calm and a sense of peace and tranquility had taken over every part of my body. Suddenly, I realized that I was standing in this dark tube. Initially, it felt as if the intangible canal went on without ending.

Something in the distance caught my eye. It sparkled in the resounding darkness and I understood that that would be the end of the tunnel. Did I really believe that while my body lay on the operating table as a surgeon removed tumorous mass from my brain, my spirit had alighted from it?

At this point, I knew there was something very powerful happening with me and I was excited to see where this tunnel was going to lead me. I was now standing in this tunnel with my arms crossed on my chest looking up at the intense bright light at the end.

Was it my time? Had other family members and friends who had gone on before me passed through this tunnel too? While I pondered on those questions, I began moving.

I had my arms crossed and it felt as I was being sucked up into this tunnel. I kept going up for some time. I moved in the direction of the light. My feet weren't how I was moving.

I kept going up for some time before I figured it out. While thinking about my family who may have passed through this very darkness and into the light, my thoughts veered in the direction of the family that lived. Currently, they were all gathered in the waiting room of the hospital.

I cannot explain the feelings and emotions that take control of our thoughts and actions at this stage of going to heaven but it is like they are automatically built into our soul and that we know what to do as if this is all programmed into each and every one of us at a much earlier time in our lives.

I knew exactly what to do but I was confused about how I knew all this information. No sooner I thought that, a burst of movement occurred. I shot upward, which made me pause and think about what had just happened. It would seem as if the more you thought about going home, the faster you went up this tunnel.

That meant I wasn't thinking of the house I lived in when I thought of home. Instead, I – and others who had come before me – had been thinking one thing: heaven = home! As thoughts and questions crowded my mind, it got to the point that I completely stopped thinking about moving up the tunnel.

I noticed that there is no physical effort. It is all done with our minds. The harder we think about going to heaven, the faster we go up this black tunnel. I looked around to find out that I had actually stopped. At this time, I noticed something else. I could reach out on both sides of me. I tested out my theory and spread out my arms. My hands and my forearms had disappeared into this black cloud. I was in a tube about 3 feet in diameter made of a black cloud. That was evident to me as soon as I focused very hard at this matter into which my body was immersed.

After zooming through the tunnel at the speed of light, I finally traversed its length, and reached the end. When I stepped out, it should have taken me a couple of minutes to get used to the light. But I didn't require any such adjustment period. I raised my hands in front of my eyes to confirm that my eyes worked fine.

This was when it hit me; I no longer had a body. I had a body while traveling up the tunnel because I was putting my hands into the black cloud that surrounded me. When I exited the tunnel, my body had transformed into what I can easily explain as a white puff of smoke or a white cloud. I did not have a body. I don't know exactly when this transformation took place but it did.

I wasn't even remotely human but like a cloud or a spirit. But all the worry left me in a hurry when I looked straight ahead of me. The reason was that I was absolutely amazed at what I was seeing.

Chapter 3: Heaven: What to Expect When You Arrive

I had exited this tunnel and was standing in a large field of the brightest yellow daisies I had ever seen. I could not see any borders or boundaries in this field of daisies. The field was completely flat. The daisies were spread as far as the eye could see. I had noticed suddenly that I had become completely overwhelmed with the feeling of Peace, Love and Tranquility.

I was completely at peace and satisfaction. While I was being amazed by the beauty of this field I had noticed I was like a cloud.

My body looked like a puff of smoke. I was actually hovering over these daisies while looking down upon them. That's when I had noticed a spirit standing in these daisies just to the left of the exit of the tunnel, he was pointing with his left arm towards the center of the field. That's when I had noticed a lonely tree in the center of this field of daisies. The tree looked to be several miles away. I then understood that this is where he wanted me to go.

Within seconds I had reached the tree and was overwhelmed by the size and the age of this old oak tree. It had to be thousands of years old. I was touching the bark of this tree still while hovering just above the daisies. I looked down to see where the tree went into the ground but the flowers grew right up to the bark of the tree and I couldn't see the base of the tree.

I was facing the tree and it was only then that I realized its true bulk and size. The oak tree for I could easily tell its species was extremely large in both height and girth. The tree was about 20 feet wide. Its branches were covered with Spanish moss. On the right side of the tree, a branch that was about 5 feet round grew. The wooden limb stretched out for about 25 yards, running parallel with the ground before shooting up.

I felt lost in the magnificence of the arboreal specimen. My gaze ran up its bark all the way to the tip of the tallest branch. That was how I found myself noticing the sky. To my utter amazement, it was a marvel that I could even liken it to a sky because it had absolutely none of the characteristics that a sky should have. We are used to blue skies with cotton wool like clouds or at least white wisps of cloudiness crisscrossing across them. But that wasn't what I saw above me now.

This sky was completely white. There was no color lent by the clouds at all either. There was no sun either; just the brightest white that I have ever seen. Again, I marveled at the whiteness being this bright but still not hurting my eyes.

While I continued my observation of the sky – yes that is what I had decided to call it even if it was drastically alien to the skies that I was used to – a spirit darted out of it. I had noticed that this spirit looked exactly like the clouds that it had just exited from and it left a trail of clouds behind it for a short distance. It was moving very fast and I can tell it was on some kind of a mission and this mission was me. One second ago, it hadn't been there and then suddenly it was! I hadn't even begun to get over my shock when I saw that it was headed in my direction. Calmly, I searched for any fear or anxiety that I should have felt.

But no, I didn't feel threatened at all. I just stood there and watch the specter fly right up to my face. Sure, I was a bit startled since it was now looking right into my eyes. The saying that our eyes are the windows to our soul sprang to mind when the spirit viewed me through mine. At that moment, I felt the old adage to be absolutely true.

The spirits eyes locked right onto mine but it is more than just a way to look at you. Because within an instant, you know what they are thinking and they can read your thoughts. This takes place without either of you ever speaking a word. When we locked eyes with each other, I could tell this

56

time I was faced with a female spirit. But I didn't know who she was.

As I maintained the eye contact, a bond connected me to her. Feelings and emotions traveled the length of that link in both directions. I knew that while I gleaned information about her, she was doing the same with me.

Her aura gave off the air of being very busy. Even so, she had stopped and conversed me in a patient way. She remained that way throughout our conversation. She had focused and concentrated very hard while looking into my eyes.

After she finished reading my mind and had received all the information she was looking for in my soul, she had then relaxed and backed off from me. She had known everything about me in a matter of 30 seconds. She then moved upward into the branches of the tree while looking down at me.

Painting by Richard DiGia

After I was used to the sudden bombarding of information about the person in front of me, I was better able to talk *to* her instead of having to work out the details myself. The spirit told me that I would have to go back. When I looked at her, she explained that it wasn't my time to go to the heavenly kingdom yet.

She must have felt reluctance gather inside of me at the thought of leaving this peaceful place. That's why she expounded that the heavenly Father wanted me to do work for Him. While I knew I was being honored in a way, few believers have been honored, I still wasn't sure that I wanted to go back.

As I relayed this message, I told her bodies were heavy, and they hurt. She fully understood what I had meant by this as she herself had experienced what it is like to be in our body form. She explained that when it was my time, this is where I will be coming.

But I knew that it will be on their terms, definitely not mine. They know when it is our time to go to heaven. I shook my head, still unconvinced, and explained my dilemma in the simplest of terms I could have. I was dreading this moment the entire time because I knew it was going to be very painful to return to my body.

I felt her nod through our connection and then she mentioned how she was passionate for all of us that are here on earth. Angels in heaven have much sympathy for us on earth and they completely understand that we are suffering here. But life is a process that we must all complete.

Chapter 4: What is Expected of You

Then the angel and I stood under the unusual tree on heavenly grounds and communicated. She explained to me our true purpose as decreed by the Heavenly Father. It shouldn't come as a surprise that she told me what our Heavenly Father truly wanted from us all, was that we love each other. It didn't shock me either!

She also added another important message from High Above as well: that we should help each other while we were alive in the world below and he does not want us to judge each other.

According to the angel, He didn't want us to compete with each other for survival. While this might go against everything that we had been taught by the so-called gurus and life coaches, it seemed to make sense. That He wanted us to live in peace was a lovely notion, especially now that wherever you turned, there was only war, violence, and famine. Children were dying and men were killing each other for no reason other than they coveted what the other person had.

As such thoughts swirled inside my head, the angel continued to tell me that Heavenly Father's idea was a world where we were all equal. After all, we are all His children and not one of us are any better than another. Beauty was God-granted as were intelligence and business acumen. Yet we continued to strut around absurdly proud of achievements that weren't really even on our own.

He also didn't want us to want things for ourselves. And I thought, the materialistic urge that caused us to plunder, thieve, steal, and kill was the root of most evils. If we understood that we weren't here to make piles out of stuff that didn't even matter, maybe we would be much nicer to each other. The angel said that the main thing that He really wanted from us is for us to love each other and help others more than we helped ourselves. It got me thinking some more. The planet hadn't been given to us segregated, but we had chosen to create distances between ourselves and other. If it wasn't race that we were fighting about, then we were cross at each other over national, religious, and even local matters. What had we made of the world that the Lord had so lovingly created for us?

It was then realization truly hit me, everything was connected and there was a reason for all that had befallen me so far. If I hadn't fallen down by the road just as I had, the doctors would never have discovered what was in my head. Had I never visited the hospital or had the surgery, I wouldn't have arrived where I was. Would I have gone through my life unknowingly ignorant of what He wanted from us all?

But that wasn't everything. The story wasn't complete yet because now I came to what had to happen after all this. My time on earth wasn't done by any means. I would have to go back. I looked at the tranquil environment that I was standing in now. It seemed alien to my own nature that I had been so afraid to come to this place. And yet now that I had arrived at the destination, I was highly reluctant to leave. But I knew that I would have to return and the main reason for me to come back to the world was going to be spreading what I had learned here. This changed everything! But who was going to believe me?!

After I returned down there, I would have to communicate with people and pass the message along. I would be letting them know that God is indeed in the heavenly kingdom and this is what He expects of us. But to do that, I would need a lot of help from the spirits. Would I be given that assistance?

The heavenly father is the only judge in this universe and when we are all individually judged by him, He will not care about how much money we made or how nice of cars we drove or what kind house we lived in. The way He will judge us is by how many and how often we helped others. This is what He will be concerned with the most.

He wants us to help each other without expecting nothing in return. That may be very hard to imagine for some people, and I can understand that. But I honestly believe this is the reason why we are all here on earth together...To be tested for our day of judgment by our Heavenly Father.

This is about the time that while I was communicating with the spirit, at a distance to my right, I had noticed a small pond of clouds in the daisies. In this pond of clouds were six spirits standing and looking down while they seemed to be swaying back and forth. They seemed to be looking for something in these clouds. Every so often, they would bend down and pull another spirit out of these clouds. Then this spirit would embrace it in its arms and somewhat cradle it gently, then fly up into the clouds above.

Painting by Richard DiGia

Then another spirit would fly out of the clouds very fast from above and take its place in the pond and continue looking down. This went on for some time, and I was trying to figure out what was going on. I eventually asked the angel what they were doing over there, and she told me they were watching hospitals and very sick people, but they do not intervene with their illnesses. They have a very high respect and concern for these doctors who are helping people on earth but again, these spirits will not intervene with the doctor- patient relationship.

It seemed to me that these doctors that were being watched by these spirits were actually working for God himself. Whether they knew it or not, these heavenly spirits are watching the work of these doctors very patiently and closely. These angels are highly amazed at what they do to try to help and heal the very sick.

My opinion has changed completely about these doctors who dedicate their lives to helping the sick. They are looked upon by these angels as doing God's work, and they are very proud of them in the heavenly kingdom. From this day on, when I speak to or see anything that has to do with the work of these doctors, I know who is watching them very closely. These doctors would be amazed to see what I had seen. I was watching all this action in the pond of clouds and it crossed my mind for just a few seconds, are these spirits watching my doctors work on me as we speak? I don't know.

Before I could voice my question, the angel told me to go back and spread the word and not to be discouraged by people's negative judgments. She said that I had to let the people know that it wasn't punishment or a rehash of our sins that awaited us in heaven. Instead, it was love that would envelop us in its arms.

According to the angel, heaven is stronger than anything any of us had ever witnessed here on earth. That is why it was silly to be afraid of death. Because dying meant we would be on our way to heaven and that should be seen as a privilege. We went to a much better place after dying. A place that wasn't anything like here.

It was the unselfish nature of the objective that was set before that convinced me to go back. All God wanted was to provide us with an even better and sweeter way to exist. And down there, we thought otherwise. We all went through our lives fearing death like it was the end of everything. As if there would be no more living once we ceased to exist down there. Instead, we would end up here and continue to exist but in a different way.

Just as certain as I was that this was my mission in life, I was also sure that going back wouldn't be easy for me. In fact, it was going to hurt and that was what I told her. I didn't know how I knew it was going to be very painful to return but somehow

I was very positive about this thought being very true. Then this heavenly being swathed in light and grace looked at me and I felt sympathy travel down the connection that we shared. She might not have had a face in the traditional sense of the word, and yet that is what I felt from her. Those huge big blue eyes looked deeply into my eyes and conveyed that message very clearly.

I felt much better about my journey back to my body because she had then told me that I would be protected. I no longer feared anything in the future from this point on because the angel just told me that I would be protected. I didn't know exactly what this protection was but I felt very safe from this moment on and nothing could hurt me. I knew at this time my operation was going to be a success. We both knew that our conversation was finished, and she had completed her mission on convincing me to go back. I, then, watched her fly straight up into the tree never to dodge a branch, like a puff of smoke. She went right through all the branches and leaves and disappeared into the clouds above.

Okay, I thought, so it was decided that I would be going back. But how will I manage that? Would I go back in the same manner that I had come? I looked around but didn't see the looming entrance of the tunnel anywhere close.

So before my brain could latch on that worry, I decided to focus on something more important. After all, if the angel was sending me back, she would already have found a way on how to do it. It shouldn't be something for me to ponder over. This wasn't anything that I had ever seen let alone experienced.

I wanted to take this time to ingrain every bit into my brain. I wished to remember as many things as I could and cast my gaze around to see as much as I could. If you want to get an idea of what I was going through, cast your mind back to a good dream that you have had. Don't you wish to commit all its details into your memory? That is what I wanted to do as well.

But being human that I was, other things intruded into my quiet speculation. I suddenly realized that I had no clue about how long I had been here. How much time had passed? There was no way to tell whether it had been a hundred years or just a few heartbeats.

Then I noticed that I wasn't breathing. I had no heartbeat. Besides the unusual nature of my breathing function, I prodded inside my head to determine what I was feeling. Curiously, neither did I feel sad nor was I mad. What was even more surprising was that I didn't have any urge to eat or satiate my thirst. It seemed that those concerns limited to the life down below. To me it looked like that nobody ate or drank in heaven.

I also noticed that there weren't any bugs on the flowers or bees or cobwebs. There seemed to be a complete absence of insects. There were no birds or butterflies either. Neither was there a wind blowing or a sun illuminating the landscape.

We all existed in a tranquil state where everything was very calm and silent. My body didn't tremble because of the cold nor was I sweating because it was too hot.

When I had come back and tried to explain to others what I experienced, all these points weren't difficult to get across. What *was* hard was trying to make them understand that there was no time where I had gone. Nobody in heaven times the ticking seconds as they pass. I happen to think that is the reason why life is so fast here on earth. For now, I knew I was going back and it was going to hurt.

I had been right because coming back had hurt really badly. I don't remember how I returned, just that my body hit something with such force and at such speed that it felt like I had just fallen off a 10 story building only to land flat on my back on cement! I did not know how I was getting back to my body but somehow I knew with no doubt that it was going to hurt very much.

Chapter 5: Down to Earth

When I woke up in the recovery room, I noticed that I was in the hospital bed. My eyes didn't fall on my nearest and dearest as they opened after surgery. They landed on a bunch of monitor screens. My head was wrapped very tight. It was like as if it was trying to expand and swell and the wrapping was stopping it from doing so. I was instantly overcome with the constant battle with pain. It was a pain that I had never experienced before in my life.

A jerky movement made me aware of all the wires and needles that were attached to my body. That was when I noticed a young man sitting across the hall behind a pane of glass. Even from this side of the glass window, I could feel his glance on me. All the observing and deducing had tired me out.

My brain gave the command and I just fell asleep as my body healed itself in the background.

Every time I opened my eyes, the man I saw before would first look at the monitors in his room and then, he would look at me. I realized then what the man was up to – he was monitoring me! The smooth way with which he raised his gaze to mine unfailingly each time made something else clear: the man knew exactly when I would be waking up. Knowing that wasn't enough to keep me awake; I kept sliding back into healing sleep.

After about 5 or 6 times that I had woken up, I opened my eyes this time and the man wasn't there. Immediately, my attention transferred to the hair on my arms. I had noticed that it was beginning to stand up like needles. At first I thought it was the medicine they were giving me through one of my I.V.s but it was more than that. There was static electricity over my entire body. I wasn't sure about the goose bumps either. It seemed that the entire room was filled with static electricity.

While monitoring the hairs on my left arm, I noticed a woman standing close by. Her huge blue eyes were squarely set on me. She had a very big smile on her face and I felt a very weird feeling of calmness and comfort upon me.

She could easily have been one of the staff or a patient's relative. But I knew she wasn't. She had long white hair that hung almost down to where her elbows began. She had on a long blue dress with a very tight collar around her neck. She was a tall thin older woman with wrinkles on her face and arms and hands. Even though the wrinkles on her face showed her age as very old, her big blue eyes were very youthful looking. I may not have recognized her or seen her before, but I was sure that she was from heaven. She had everything to do with the hair standing up on my entire body.

When she saw me looking at her and recognizing her heavenly origins, she said, "Do you know that the Heavenly Father wants you to come back and do work for Him?"

76

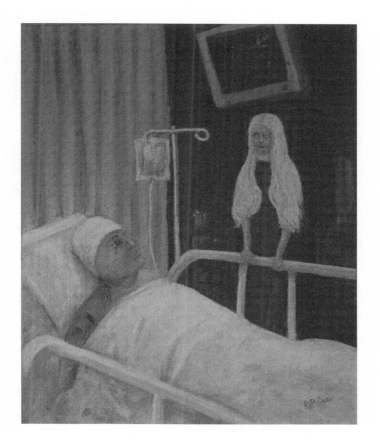

Painting by Richard DiGia

Without missing a blink, I had said "Yes. She told me that under the tree. But she didn't tell me exactly what he wants me to do."

You can see that I had failed to mention who that *she* was, but that woman hadn't required any explanations. She immediately knew who I had meant, which gave further credibility to her origins.

Then she said, "You will know when the time comes" and put one finger on my lips.

A flood of adrenalin crashed into my entire body almost immediately.

There I was, feeling as if someone had just poured 5 gallons of very cold ice water down my throat that I felt reach my toes very fast. And there she was, smiling down at me before she turned and walked to the door. I watched her turn left as realization hit me. I was now being visited by angels. That was when I understood that I no longer had anything to fear. I felt very safe from this moment on. I knew I was being watched and protected.

This was the exact moment that all the monitors started beeping. The young man came into my room, but he didn't seem worried. Instead, he looked like he was very excited and confused.

He said, "Tim you're doing great! What happened?"

I said, "I don't know." Then I asked him, "Where did that Lady go?"

His face now wore a confused expression as he asked, "What lady?"

"The lady that was just in here a minute ago?" I asked. "She had long white hair and a long blue night gown," Then I explained.

But he only said, "Tim, there is nobody in here. You are the only one in this area, but I can go look for her if you want me to."

I nodded and requested, "Sure, would you? Please?"

The man said "Okay" and left the room. First, he turned right and then I saw him go the other way.

A few heartbeats later, he re-entered the room and told me, "Tim, the doors are all locked. There is nobody here."

There were no windows in this room, and there was no clock, so I had no idea what time of the day this had taken place.

At that time, I understood that I hadn't been dreaming. Reassured in what I had seen, I then went back to sleep. The next time I woke up, I had been shifted to a different room. This time though, I was surrounded not by inanimate objects but, by all my family members. They were all excited for me because I had pulled through the operation. I wanted to join them, but I was in so much pain that I just laid there and clinched my legs tightly. I ground my teeth down because of the agonizing, intense pain. . I would deny any pain medicine when asked because I wanted to be fully aware of another visit from the angels.

One morning, I woke up to find that there was a man sitting on the left side of my bed. I took my time to take in his appearance. The stranger had black curly hair and was wearing a brown sports jacket with patches on the elbows and brown pants. He was holding a clip board in his hands, and was sitting there, as if waiting for me to wake up. I found out later that that really had been the case!

When I did wake up finally, he told me that he worked with all the hospitals in this area. That was simple and straightforward enough.

But the next question that he asked wasn't as simple! The man asked me whether I had gone anywhere during my operation. Now, you can understand my trepidation. Even though, I didn't want to lie to him, I didn't know this guy. What I had seen and experienced had changed me and my life forever. That much was true. But so was the fact that it was an out-of-this-world experience.

What if I confided in this man and he thought my brain surgery had gone wrong? Thinking me insane, he would probably do his best to have me locked up. He couldn't have known that

I was telling the truth. Could he? So, what choice did I have but to deny anything out of the ordinary had happened to me? I told him no. I had gone nowhere during the surgery. Like most patients, I had floated in a river of unconsciousness and only woken up afterwards.

The man didn't make it easy for me though. He was persistent to get me to talk about my experience. It seemed like he knew I had seen something mind-boggling and wanted confirmation of it. When I refused to provide him the satisfaction, he just sat there, and started tapping on his clipboard with his pencil. It looked like he wanted to wait me out until I confessed. I gave him nothing; he asked, again. This time, he wanted to know had I seen anything in the Afterlife or talked to anyone?

I gave him a skeptical look to strengthen my case and responded, "What, like aliens?"

He then explained to me the real purpose of his presence. According to the man, people like me, i.e., those who have had this type of surgery had stories to tell when the anesthesia wore off. So, he said, he would very much like to hear mine, if I had one.

I again said, "Nope, I have nothing to tell. No stories to spin. I just went to sleep and then I woke up. That's all."

The man looked at me for a minute and then stood up. His hand dipped into the front pocket of his shirt and came out holding a business card. He handed it to me and said to please call him, if I happened to remember anything at all. I took the card and then said okay, I would.

What I didn't let him see was that I could tell he was upset with me. It was clear that he wasn't buying what I was selling because he knew something was up. But since calling me a liar outright wouldn't have convinced me to share my story with him, the man didn't have any options. So, he chose to leave and give me some time to reconsider. When he had gone, I crumpled the card in my hand and dropped it in the garbage without even looking at it.

In my head, thoughts circled and I decided that I had better not tell anyone my story.

There were now two reasons that I could think of that prevented me from telling anyone. One, I knew that many people wouldn't realize that I was telling the truth and think of me as having gone insane. And more importantly, two, because people will judge.

I knew that judging other people is wrong and the Heavenly Father does not want people to judge others by any means. I felt at that moment I was already being tested by what the spirit was trying to explain to me under the tree, how people judge others in many different ways.

Even though, at that time, I knew there was something very special going on with my life and that I was being protected by these angels. I knew there was pain here on earth and we experience that every minute while we are in our bodies. That

84

the situation might have taken a different turn had I chosen to confide in that stranger. I needed help and I went to an expert for advice.

My family is Catholic, so my first thought was to confront the priest of the church that we regularly visited. When we met, I told him my story. I didn't leave anything out from going to heaven to what I had done there and what I had learned. The priest was very understanding towards me.

Instead of rebuking me for spouting lies or calling me insane, the man of God and I bonded closely on this matter.

He seemed to be able to relate with my story, which was a pleasant surprise since he had never been where I had gone. But he did tell me he had heard stories about people going to heaven and standing under this large oak tree in the daisies. He also told me that my experiences with these angels will continue for the rest of my life and that I am a very special individual to be chosen.

He wanted to hear about any further experiences I might encounter with the angels. I had returned several times after this to explain my encounters and they were very pleased that I had shared these stories with them. I felt at this time, the priests were the only ones I could talk to about my experiences.

The priest talked to me for a bit and then had recommended that I write a book to let people know of my experience. It would not only spread the message to other people, just like the angel had suggested.

A book might also connect me to others who had had a similar experience. While it was sage advice and I respected the person who imparted it to me, I did not feel right about taking it.

That's because I have always been somewhat a private person. I knew that there were things going on in my life that I could not explain. But did that mean I was ready to shout out the secret to the world? I was very confused at this point because I was being pulled from my comfort zone of life. I kept thinking about what the angel wanted me to do. Tell as many people as I can about what heaven is like and what the heavenly father wants from all of us but not to be discouraged by others negative judgment.

This was very hard for me and I didn't know how to do this. Did I want to share it with people who might judge me, ridicule me, or simply not believe me? No! I don't think I had yet arrived at that place. So, I refused.

Adding to the events that were complicating my life was the fact that I couldn't work the way I used to. It translated into frustration and becoming upset with myself.

Consequently, I had started feeling down. But, it was as if a pleasant distraction had already been planned to take off my mind from things that I couldn't help. Because it was about the time that my oldest son, Timothy, had his first baby. Timothy's son was named Tristan Anthony Peak at his birth. He was born on November 6th 2014 and since Tristan was our very first grandchild, my excitement at his impending arrival knew no bounds!

But Tristan didn't make a smooth transition into our world. He was born pre-mature, which meant that we had to wait for a month before we could bring him home.

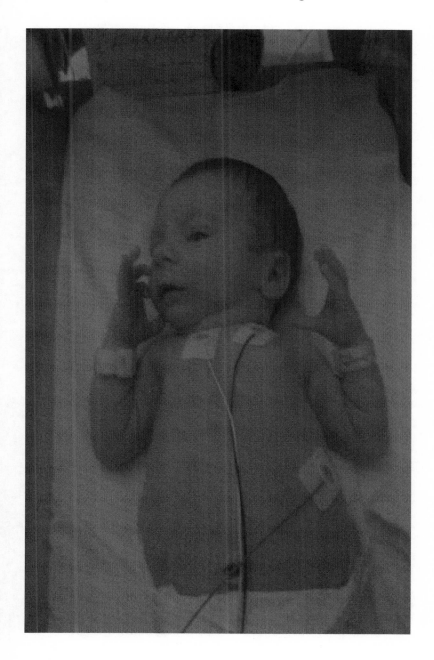

For as long as Tristan was kept in the hospital after being born, we visited him every day. The doctors pronounced Tristan healthy enough to come home and our excitement reached new heights.

In all our excitement, we had his bedroom all fixed up and waiting for his arrival. When he finally came home to us, he was the life of all of the family. I held a miracle in my hands and it made me so happy! I thanked God for the beautiful gift that He had given to me and my family. Tristan had entered our lives like a breath of fresh air.

It was the best thing that had happened to my family in a long, long time. Personally, I had needed Tristan's presence in my life at that time, which was why I thanked God for him every day. I went to Tristan's house almost every day. Picking him up and playing with him had quickly become one of my favorite ways of passing time.

One day, I had been sitting on the swing that my father had built and installed in the back yard. I held Tristan in my arms and the child was cooing in that insanely adorable way of babies. Since it had started getting dark, I brought him into the house. It wasn't just me whom Tristan had wrapped around his tiny finger. Everyone wanted to hold him and play with him all the time.

It was the same on that day. Our family played with Tristan on my parent's living room floor. My wife gave him a bath, and got his pajamas on. He looked so fragile that we handled him with immense care and a gentle touch. Together, as grandparents we want to pamper our grandkids.

Then, I put him in his car seat. Everyone kissed him goodbye.

Tristan was going for his first wagon ride in the neighborhood the next morning and his grandpa would be taking him. Everyone was so excited the way we used to get no matter what he did. Whether it was his first smile or first sneeze, we all would fall in love with him all over again. I put Tristan in the car. We drove to his parents' place where his mother Amanda was waiting for us on the back porch.

On his arrival, she was as excited to see him as if he had been gone from her for years. I completely understood because that was exactly the way I felt when I saw him each day! She took him out of his car seat and embraced him with overwhelming love, hugs and kisses.

As I handed Tristan to Amanda, I remember telling her that I would be back in the morning. She looked at me and I explained that it was so I would get him to take him on his first wagon ride. Amanda smiled and told me that she thought that would be great. She then took him into the house with such a big smile on her face.

We are told that love has no bounds, and that it can take many forms. Indeed, there is no stronger bond than the love between a mother and her child. You just feel the immense power of love and sacrifice exuding from a mother. It is also often seen that kids would quiet down (from crying) the minute they are held within their mother's embrace. I guess the babies sense that warmth and love and the feeling of being sheltered.

To all of us in the family, including myself, Tristan was the most beautiful thing we had ever seen. He was our personal tiny miracle. But he didn't stay with us for long.

Chapter 6: The Day Our Lives Took a Turn

On the same night, we were in bed when my wife hurriedly sat up in bed. Her movements jostled me awake as well. I looked at the time and the clock said it was 3 am. I sat up to make sure she was all right.

An ominous feeling hung in the air around us, a feeling of something bad happening. My wife's next words only added to the feeling. She said she heard sirens and something was wrong with the baby. Before I could even attempt to coax her back to sleep, she had jumped up out of bed.

I watched her run downstairs surprised at the depth of her feelings. It was like her motherly senses were running at a full pace. Even I felt stabs in my aura. The skin on my arms prickled and that was when I looked down. The hair on my arms was standing up and goose bumps dotted the terrain of my arms.

I knew then that my wife's premonitory panic had, unfortunately, been spot on. My lips formed the words, oh no not the baby...God! By that time, my wife had returned upstairs. She had put her coat on and was ready to leave. Let's go! She beckoned to me and I was able to put my panic on hold...at least for the time being.

My son lived nearby; his place is right up the street from mine. We were never really apart even if we lived in separate houses. I have never been gladder of the lack of distance between our places of residence than when I was that night. If there was even a hint of any kind of trouble, it didn't take us long to go running to their help. That is what happened that night. My wife and I ran out the door in the wake of the screaming sirens.

The ambulance led us right to my son's house. It *was* the baby. Little Tristan, the apple of our eyes whom we all loved so dearly, had died of SIDS that night.

I will never forget that this happened on April 12th 2015 because each detail from that night is etched into my mind. Imagine just spending 5 months with a child who had defied the odds right from the start because that's how old Tristan had been when he passed away.

He had had a difficult birth, but had managed to come through it. He managed to go through all the pain and tribulations and to give hope to his parents of being blessed with nurturing a child. He tried his best, but then *this* had happened.

Emotions welled up inside me. But quickly surpassing it was anger. I gradually realized that I was mad and not at myself, my wife, or my son's family. No, I was mad at God! Inside my head, the questions, Why God? Why did you take the baby? Why? Why was he made to go through all the pain at birth when this was to become of him? If he was to be taken away from us, then why was he given to us in the first place? I kept repeating these questions to myself over and over again.

It was making me even angrier to see how my whole life had been completely devastated within a matter of minutes! How could happiness and love become so cruel so quickly? How can such a pleasant and heart-warming gift be taken from us in mere moments?

We began to revolve our lives around him; our every activity had him in the loop. We used to schedule our routine according to his needs. Tristan was all there was. And for him to be taken from us like that, was heartless and not the work of the "loving God".

I wanted to give God a piece of my mind and I knew just where I could do that. Of course, none of us slept much that night. We just passed the time enveloped in immense grief. We would comfort each other when they begin to lose composure and in return, they did the same for us.

We tried to be there for each other as much as we could. But it was only superficial. We all were carrying separate grieves. We all had different equations with Tristan and no matter what we say to each other and what we do for each other, the pain of losing him would not be compensated for or relieved.

The emotions were boiling up inside me. I had to vent it. I had to find a thing a, person on whom I can release the lava that was erupting inside me. And just as soon as morning arrived I headed straight to the priest. The same man of God with whom I had shared my visit to heaven with.

I walked into his office and started yelling at him as if it had been he who had personally offended me. I asked him why God had taken the baby. Why had he taken him away from his loved ones? From the very people that took immense care of him? I kept asking him at an insanely high pitch. And the man remained calm and composed.

He calmly said, "Tim, God doesn't take people. Things on earth happen and we go to God. God didn't take baby Tristan."

The thing is that I was hurting so terribly at that moment, that those weren't the words I wanted to hear. Those words made me much angrier than I was before. They did not do anything to soothe my anger. Even though, the priest was just being kind to me, I guess I didn't want to hear any explanations he had. There was only one thing that would have made me step out of my grief at that moment. We just wanted the baby back in our arms. We wanted to hold Tristan again and live our lives around him.

But that was something that I didn't know how to make happen. A sense of helplessness washed over me. Now I was not only thinking about myself, but my wife and children also. Because I came across the intensity of how I was feeling, it made me realize that my family would be feeling as much with more intensity, perhaps. I could not think straight. There was a plethora of emotions that washed over me again and again and I could not decide which train of thought to follow. Just as the emotions came over me with intensity, they ended up draining me and making me numb.

Eventually, his gentle manner and kind words did calm me down a bit. However, while I had relented enough to listen to the priest, it hadn't lessened my anger at God. Inside, I was still very angry with God. You see, it wasn't just Tristan who had died that night. He had been the beating heart for his parents. Their lives came to a standstill that night. Since my wife and I loved our son and his family with all our heart, it was as if we had stopped existing too. Tristan took away the life of the whole family with him. We buried baby Tristan on my birthday, April 15th.

That day was probably the most challenging for my family to live through. We had a mass in St. Vitus church for Tristan's funeral. He was buried on top of my grandfather in the catholic cemetery. Afterwards, we became used to the grief we carried around with us. Becoming used to might make it sound like it became an everyday thing for us. But it was not like this. We woke up every day with a thought of having to live without Tristan. He remained in our thoughts all the time. But life did sputter and start for us again.

However, my son and his wife are still walking around today unable to understand what happened to their baby. For parents whose baby was just 5 months old, it can be especially difficult to move on. For mother especially, as she nurtured the child for nine months in her womb. Both of them had create an inimitable bond with their child. My son and his girlfriend could not go back to their house for weeks because of the babies belongings still throughout the house. Watching all those belongings would send them down the same emotionally challenging pathway which they encountered at the time of Tristan's death.

However, I took it upon myself to do it for them. I dreaded going to the house and boxing all the toys, clothes, swings, crib and furniture and taking them from the house. One morning I did just that and it was one of the hardest things I have ever done. I boxed half and put them in my truck and I couldn't do any more. I explained my situation to my father and he had returned alone to finish. It's a very sad situation and I wish that no parent should ever have to go through it.

About two months after Tristan had left us, my wife and my son Tyler went for a ride to Beaufort, South Carolina. We visit the Hunting Island State Park often. We find the ambiance peaceful and the place beautiful. We thought that some time away from where we had experienced such a huge loss would help us get our lives back together.

It was the middle of the day and we were a few miles down the street in Port Royal. It was turning out to be a beautiful day. There wasn't a cloud in the sky! I was looking for a gas station. When I found one, I could tell right away that it had newly opened because the first thing I had noticed about it were its new gas pumps and a shiny new parking lot. Coupled with the newness was the fact that the service building was pretty far from the pumps. Besides, we couldn't see any cars filling up or even parked in the lot. That's why my wife and I were wondering if it was even open.

However, we were still at some distance from the pump during these observations. I decided to pull up and when I reached closer to the pumps, we could see that the lights were on inside. So, I parked and got out of the truck. I had pulled up right next to the pump, which is why I didn't think twice before I left my door open.

Standing outside, I looked around, and something told me that everything wasn't right here. What kind of gas station doesn't have even one person going about their business? Why were there no cars parked or pulling up just as we had? Shaking my head at the mystery that was as of yet unsolved, I swiped my card, and the pump turned on.

As I began fueling, I leaned against my truck. Just then the hair on my arms began to stand up. Having experienced the most unusual things ever since my surgery, my response was oh, now what! It turns out that was exactly the right response to have at that moment. Because who would come into view but two girls. I watched them as they seemed to materialize from somewhere around the back of my truck. They wore long flowing dresses of blue that swept the ground so low that you couldn't see their feet. My eyes fell on the tight collars that the dress formed around their necks. Their long blond hair swanned around them and they just smiled as they walked towards me. Huge, very blue eyes and a complexion that was white like paper formed the last of my observations. By then, they had reached me.

One of them commanded my attention by saying, "Excuse me, can I speak to you please?"

You might not be surprised at this time that I knew right away who these girls were.

The same girl continued to talk and she said to me, "You've had a death in your family recently. Haven't you?"

If their appearance hadn't caught me by surprise, you can guess that their odd question didn't either.

I nodded and said "Yes, the baby."

That is all I said, as if I knew they'd understand that I was referring to Tristan. I mean, this was the first time I was meeting them. The girl talking to me reached out with her arm. In her dainty hands, she held a card. The card had a picture of Jesus on it – one where He had His arms spread out, showing His palms.

While I was looking at the card, the girl had asked me, "Could you do me a favor please?"

I found my head was already nodding an affirmative before I could say "Yes."

The mysterious girl said, "Could you please tell the parents of that 5-month-old baby not to be sad?"

There, it was confirmed now that she had known who I had been talking about, just as I had instinctively known who she and the other girl were.

"He knows that they are sad and He doesn't want them to be sad," she had finished saying.

My mind was now a jumble of questions. Now that there was a receptacle or a way to communicate with Him, there were so many things I wanted to ask about sweet Tristan's early parting with us. But they weren't all as important as the question that I asked.

Because the very first thing I said to her after her small speech was, "Why didn't God let me heal the baby, so he didn't die?"

She responded with "Only the Divine Ones can do that."

Unsurprisingly, at that time, I had no idea who the Divine Ones were.

But she had more to say, "He is very happy and he is a saint in the heavenly kingdom. He is sitting at the right hand of the heavenly father. He doesn't want those parents to be sad."

We were worried because baby Tristan was not baptized before he died. We were in the process of doing so but his death was before this had happened. The priest had told us that infants have a free pass to heaven but we were still concerned with this. It was then confirmed to me after the talk with these angels. The priest was right.

Since there was still so much that I didn't understand, I just nodded and said, "I will tell them."

Then the girl said, "There is one other thing that you'd need to tell the parents of that 5-month-old baby. Can you tell them that they can raise him as an infant when they go to the Heavenly Kingdom?"

I looked at them, but there was nothing that I could have said to either one of those girls that would have surprised them. Nothing that would change the serene expression on their faces. They just stood there and smiled the entire time.

My mind was brimming with many questions that I was desperately looking for answers for and I thought that I was finally going to get answers.

This meeting I had with them meant that I had a message to deliver even if I was still struggling to come to terms with Tristan's passing away. So, I turned around and gave the card to my wife who was still in the truck.

She seemed surprised and said, "Who are those girls?"

I told her that they were talking about the baby! At that, I turned around to introduce them to my wife. But by then, they were gone.

Apparently, the girls had disappeared just as suddenly as they had arrived. They had a message to get across and once their job was done, they had left. I looked around for them. My wife, too, got out of the truck and helped me look for them. But they were nowhere to be found. I hadn't a clue as to where they had gone. My gaze fell on the pump and

I quickly turned it off. The pump's meter displayed $44.30.

That was the only thing I could think about until I got home. Then I told my son what had happened. Understandably, he was confused about what was going on. Even today he thinks that God has done something very cruel to him and he still is not able to adjust his life like it was before the baby's death. He still wants his baby boy back very desperately so much so that he wants to go to heaven just to be with him. It is a very sad situation. My other two sons had babies recently. Jordan has a beautiful, healthy boy named Isaac, and Spencer has a beautiful, healthy girl named Adrianna. They are both so special to us!

My oldest son has a hard time being around them because Isaac looks so much like Tristan. It is heartbreaking to witness how badly my son and his girlfriend want their baby back. I still think that was the ultimate cruel fate that could ever happen to any parent.

The priest, however, told us to thank God for letting us have Tristan. We were blessed to enjoy him for the five months that he was here with us. He said he could have died at birth and we would have never even experienced his love for those 5 months! But I still think it was very wrong. It just doesn't make any sense to me. I think about him all the time and we really miss him.

Chapter 7: On Earth: What was Expected from Me

My grief aside, my duties here on Earth had just begun. It was during another trip to Lowes that I had my next out-of-this-world experience. I had gone there to get a piece of glass cut. At a shop, there was a very nice man who had waited on me. He told me his name was Fred. I watched him cutting the glass while I leaned against a shelf in his shop. Without warning, all the hair on my arms stood up.

Since I didn't know this man at all, I was trying to figure out what to say to him.

I chose to say, "There is something wrong with you. Isn't there?"

Fred looked up at me and put his tools down. Then he told me that he had had a liver transplant a year ago. I nodded when he confirmed what my instincts had been telling me.

I told him to go to the doctor because something was wrong. Fred agreed to do that and that was that. Until a couple months later when I ran into him again. I had gone back there and Fred came running up to me. He told me he wanted to thank me for telling him to go to the doctor back then.

Tests revealed that part of his liver was failing, which was why he had to have another operation. But Fred assured me that he was doing fine now. Then hesitantly, he had asked me how I had known what I did. My answer took him by complete surprise. I told him that it was a gift.

While the doctor had been right about my life being different after the surgery, I thought otherwise. From the moment, I got back home my life had become much better. Even though, I had suffered physical damage to my mind and body, these events had made my brain much stronger.

About a week or two later, I was in the same store rushing through the Isle to purchase a part when I had noticed the hair on my arms standing up again.

I stopped in my tracks and looked around. I didn't see anything that caught my attention. I then took two steps back and noticed a man looking at tools. I then turned and walked towards him.

I had no idea why I was going up to this man. When I got up to him I stood next to him and we both were looking at the same tools side by side. I still didn't know what I was doing there. I was looking at his boots then I looked at him and he looked up at me. We both said hello and as soon as I looked at his face I told him there's something wrong with his left eye and he needs to go to the doctors right away.

He said he had cancer behind his eye, and he had just finished chemo about two months ago and he was told the cancer was all gone.

I told him that the cancer isn't gone and he needs to go back to the doctors right away. He asked me how I knew that and I told him that it was a gift. He went to the doctors the next day and was told the cancer was back again and they continued the chemo again. I saw this man again after this ordeal. His name is Shawn and he thanked me for telling him what I had told him. He then said the cancer was all gone this time.

I might have lost in one sense, but I had also gained much more in another. I have changed for the better. As I had been told to do, I don't judge people. I help as many people as I can. While I never lied to, cheated, stole, or deceived people even before my heavenly visit, I took even more care not to do so now.

All that I do is because I feel that I need to keep up with my part of the agreement I had made with God. I know that He intervened with my life and it turned me into a much calmer person. Besides, now I know that nothing we do on this earth matters. The only thing that does is that we should do well with our lives and understand what God expects from us. If we succeed at it, we will be rewarded with the best gift of all. I am, of course, talking about an eternal life with our Creator in the heavenly kingdom.

Just the other day, I happened to be watching the Dr. Oz show. It was April 5, 2019. This particular day, he had a guest on his show, who was a professional neurologist, named Dr. Joel Salinas who claimed to be a mirror-touch synesthesia. He claimed to be able to predict people's illnesses.

Before my experience with the angels, I would have been very skeptical of this man's theory to be able to perform such a task. But I sat there and listened to the man's story and I believe 100% that this man is capable of performing this duty in life.

In my own personal experience, I strongly believe that this doctor is being used by these angels to do God's work. He is a very special person who has been chosen by these angels for some reason to use these capabilities to help others heal.

Scientists have done many studies and tests on the human brain, trying to come up with the answer to this special capability only to come up with unknown scientific conclusions and speculations. I don't think science has anything to do with this matter at all. I think these scientists are just grabbing at straws, trying to figure out a medical excuse behind this matter.

There was also another episode where the show had several guests on with personal experiences and encounters with angels. Each of these guests had their own story that involved angels and the doctors discussed their own personal beliefs about these encounters. Their final conclusion was that these encounters with angels do exist and they are very much true. The date of this episode was Friday, April 26th 2019.

Chapter 8: Concluding the Angelic Words

Towards the end, I have a clear hope that my experiences will help someone. I have a sincere belief that what I had gone through will serve a huge purpose for the people who are in need of the lessons I was given. God chose me to help the ones who cannot understand their grief.

Maybe someone that had a baby or a loved family member who died and so they have questions about what happens to people when they die. We are not alone after death and there is nothing to be afraid of. This chapter on earth ends and we go to God. I had witnessed many strange things after my journey, things that are very hard to explain.

It is like I have been guided to different situations for unknown reasons. I have never wrote a book before and I don't even know anyone, personally, who has. I wrote this book because I was told by the angels, so that I can give a clear explanation to the people. I guess I am just the messenger.

For about a decade, I had thought about how I was going to spread the word of my experience and I had thought about this story every day since my operation. It was something that needed to be told.

I embarked upon this feat, having no previous experiences of writing, and it felt like the words appeared on their own. The writing at the end of my pen was not deliberated, rather the words seemed to be gifted to me by the higher authority.

Such is not my naïve assumption, and you would think it too when you have had the mental disability I had owed to loss of memory which in turn was caused by the tumor in my head.

I struggle every day just to remember what I had done yesterday. And at times, it can be a lot frustrating. I would feel useless as I thought that I did not have the complete control over my resources. That I was not able to put myself to good use. That I was carrying a useless vessel around that was not good for anything. I was told by the doctors to just be glad that I am alive and to enjoy every day like it was my last.

My wife had helped me in the process of this story and I probably would have had a very difficult time completing this mission because I cannot remember much that goes on throughout my day but this story was chiseled into my brain, word for word, and I told my wife that it's like I'm not the one writing this story. I believe that I am being helped by the angels I met with.

I was guided to a ghostwriting firm in California some 3,000 miles away from me and when I called them to help me publish a book, I had spoken to a very nice gentleman named Luke Shelton.

When I spoke with him, I told him my story and he was certain I had called him for a reason because he had recently had a young daughter that passed away and he was struggling with his own grief. I was still leery about going through this but Luke had insisted that I hire his firm and they will go above and beyond to help me get this book published and be seen by the world.

He found my story to be very interesting and he was persistent to help me. I told him that the angel wanted me to share my experience with as many people as I can and that this book was to be just the beginning.

Through this book, more and more people would understand what happens to us after we die. I was still skeptical after talking to Luke, not just because I wasn't sure how to go about this matter but I could not afford to write a book.

We are still struggling with medical bills and baby Tristan still doesn't have a head stone on his grave because we don't have the money.

After talking to Luke he thought it was important for me to write this book and his firm will work with me to make monthly payments during the process of this book.

I finally agreed and he then introduced me to a lovely woman named Lisa Taylor. She is one of the most patient persons I have ever met. For 5 months she had worked with me and I'm sure I had discouraged her many times but I would never know that because she definitely knows how to do her job.

Then finally, there is the actual writer who worked very hard to make this story come alive and I could only imagine what he had gone through working with me. His name is Daniel McCain. He is very professional about his work and he was very patient with me in his unique way.

I couldn't have asked for a better team of writers to put this story together to be told to the world. I basically had a very interesting story to tell and I shared it with this professional team of writers and they are the ones that did all the work to put this book together.

If anyone is considering to hire a ghostwriting firm, I would highly recommend calling Luke Shelton, Lisa Taylor and Daniel McCain at Ghostwriters LLC. I was asked by Lisa to locate some pictures that I had seen in heaven and I looked at thousands of pictures and I could not find even one to compare to what I had actually seen in heaven. Including the angels that I spoke with there.

I was guided to a local sketch artist named Richard Digia from New Castle Pa. After telling him my story he said he would be honored to paint the pictures of these angels I had seen in heaven.

Upon talking to him further about my experience, I got to know about the other occurrences that Digia had come across regarding such experiences. He told me that I wasn't Richards's first encounter that recounted to him with the experiences of having met with angels.

Upon our discussion, Richard decided to paint a few pictures for my book. The last three pictures in this book are painted by him and they probably seem foreign in a sense to what we are expected to think of heaven to look like, however, they hold an uncanny resemblance to what I had seen and witnessed.

To Heaven and Back With Angels

By Timothy Peak

This story is about an ordinary guy from Western Pennsylvania, who had a quick visit to heaven. In that visit, he was instructed by the angels to go back and inform as many people as possible about this experience in Heaven. This guy was also told to convey what the heavenly father expects from all of us here on earth. I, Timothy peak, am that guy. For 10 years I thought about this and didn't know how I was going to do this. I was told by a couple of priests at my church that a book would be a great way to get my story out there into the world. I am not a writer and never wrote a book before. My story involves visiting these angels in heaven and receiving several visits from these angels on earth. I intend for this book to help anyone with questions about our lives after death or what happens to our loved ones and our infants after they die. Suffice it to say that we are all being watched by angels every day and they truly understand our pain while we are here. Life is a mission that we must all complete before we will be judged by our heavenly father in heaven.